ISBN 978-1-330-21344-5
PIBN 10054294

This book is a reproduction of an important historical work. Forgotten Books uses state-of-the-art technology to digitally reconstruct the work, preserving the original format whilst repairing imperfections present in the aged copy. In rare cases, an imperfection in the original, such as a blemish or missing page, may be replicated in our edition. We do, however, repair the vast majority of imperfections successfully; any imperfections that remain are intentionally left to preserve the state of such historical works.

1 MONTH OF
FREE
READING

at
www.ForgottenBooks.com

By purchasing this book you are eligible for one month membership to ForgottenBooks.com, giving you unlimited access to our entire collection of over 1,000,000 titles via our web site and mobile apps.

To claim your free month visit:
www.forgottenbooks.com/free54294

English
Français
Deutsche
Italiano
Español
Português

www.forgottenbooks.com

Mythology Photography **Fiction**
Fishing Christianity **Art** Cooking
Essays Buddhism Freemasonry
Medicine **Biology** Music **Ancient
Egypt** Evolution Carpentry Physics
Dance Geology **Mathematics** Fitness
Shakespeare **Folklore** Yoga Marketing
Confidence Immortality Biographies
Poetry **Psychology** Witchcraft
Electronics Chemistry History **Law**
Accounting **Philosophy** Anthropology
Alchemy Drama Quantum Mechanics
Atheism Sexual Health **Ancient History**
Entrepreneurship Languages Sport
Paleontology Needlework Islam
Metaphysics Investment Archaeology
Parenting Statistics Criminology
Motivational

DISCOURSES

ON THE .

PHILOSOPHY OF RELIGION.

ADDRESSED

TO DOUBTERS WHO WISH TO BELIEVE.

BY GEORGE RIPLEY.

" A true philosophy in the learned class is essential to a true religious feeling in all classes."
COLERIDGE.

𝔅𝔬𝔰𝔱𝔬𝔫:

JAMES MUNROE AND COMPANY.

1836.

Entered according to the Act of Congress, in the year 1836,
By James Munroe & Co.
in the Clerk's Office of the District Court of the District of Massachusetts.

PREFACE.

THE following discourses are not published by way of controversy. Their only aim is the quickening of a pure faith in spiritual truth, by a calm exposition of some of the principles on which it rests. They were written, and preached, nearly two years since, to the people of my pastoral charge. One of them has already been given to the public,* but I think it right to introduce it here as an integral part of the whole series.

It is certain that any discourses, prepared in the usual course of professional labor, without the remotest view to publication, are likely to be found unworthy of 'a wider sphere. I am sensible that these discourses can claim little merit, except that of containing the distinct, expression of ideas, which seem to me of vital importance to the welfare of man. They are set forth in so many ways by more skilful hands than mine, that I should be ashamed of the sight of them in print, did I not feel called upon by a strong sense of duty to reveal my whole mind to those who are already in possession of one side of my faith. I have been thought by some esteemed friends to have exhibited views in a recent number of one of our theological journals† that are liable to many serious objections. I fear also that I may have unconsciously given pain to some devout and timid minds, who think that discussions of this nature serve only to unsettle the foundations of Christian faith. I have the most heartfelt

* Discourse V. Liberal Preacher, Nov. 1835.
† Christian Examiner for Nov. 1836. Review of Martineau's Lectures.

sympathy with such minds. I would sooner never speak again than do aught which tends to cloud the blessed light of a serene and confiding piety. It was my purpose, in the discussion alluded to, to suggest a mode of considering the evidences of Christianity which should free it from certain difficulties under which it has been thought to labor. No one who has read my article understandingly can suppose that I intended to cast any doubt on the reality of the Christian miracles—or that I doubted them myself. I do not. Their certainty being once established, by what I deem the only valid proof, they are no less holy and precious to me than to others.

The fears which are entertained by many, who are not theologians by profession, with regard to the effect of free discussion, often arises from the want of an intelligent and vigorous faith. They dread lest the progress of inquiry should bring to light some hidden defect in the grounds of our religion. They are, in fact, doubters, though they know it not. They wish to believe. They cannot bear to hear a word said which implies that any cherished view is wrong. But this arises from a lurking suspicion that there is something unsound in the fabric of their faith. To such minds these discourses are addressed. I would frankly point out to them the principles on which my own faith is built; and I cannot but hope that theirs will gain strength by the exposition. The interests of speculative science and of practical piety appear to me so intimately blended, that it would cause me deep sorrow to think that I had laid a rude hand on either. What I have recently published explains the negative side of my faith. I here give the positive; and one should read both the statements in connexion, in order to perceive the complete whole in which I venture to think my views exist in my own mind.

These pages do not claim to exhibit any thing new. I would watch for light from every quarter; and I can hardly suppose that my eyes are open to any rays which have not fallen on many others also. Resemblances may be detected between some of the views here advanced and those which are maintained by far abler pens. They are not intentional, but are traceable to the unconscious influence that is always exerted on a seeking mind by master spirits, which it looks up to and reverences.

I ought to ask pardon for some repetitions of thought and expression. Perhaps they are not more, however, than were to be expected in compositions prepared at intervals of several weeks, by one whose mind was possessed with a few predominant ideas. Besides, it was my purpose to present the same course of argument in two or three different applications. The attentive reader, I trust, will discover that " uniformity of thought and design which will always be found in the writings of the same person when he writes with simplicity and in earnest."*

Boston, November 18, 1836.

---

* Bishop Butler's Preface to his Sermons.

CONTENTS.

" Wisdom is the brightness of the Everlasting Light, the unspotted mirror of the Power of God and the image of his Goodness. And being but one she can do all things; and in all ages entering into holy souls, she maketh them friends of God and prophets."

DISCOURSE I.

HEBREWS xi. 27.

"FOR HE ENDURED, AS SEEING HIM WHO IS INVISIBLE."

THESE words are applied by the writer of the Epistle to the Hebrews, to the ancient lawgiver of their nation, as descriptive of the principle of faith which formed a prominent element in his character. They may be regarded as describing with no less justice and force the peculiar character of every truly religious man. For there is nothing which more strongly marks the believer in religious truth, than his firm conviction of the reality of a vast range of subjects, which do not come under the cognizance of any of the senses. His thoughts are not confined to the contemplation of facts, which are presented to the notice of the outward eye. His mind is not limited to the gross and material objects, with which he is now surrounded, but passing over the boundaries of space and time, is conversant with truths, which bear the stamp of Infinity and Eternity. He is conscious of an inward nature, which is the source of more important and comprehensive ideas, than any which the external senses suggest, and he follows the decision of these ideas as the inspir-

2

ing voice of God, with none the less confidence, because they lead him into the region of the Infinite and Invisible. The principle of faith in the truth and reality of these ideas, exerts such a strong influence over his mind, that he acts as if their objects were now present with him ; he proceeds upon their certainty, with as much assurance, as if they had been exhibited to his bodily eye ; he endures as seeing him who is invisible. This, indeed, is so obvious and essential a trait in the character of the truly religious man, that it has led those who are blind to the destiny of our nature, to charge him with being a visionary, and devoted to objects that lie beyond the cognizance of the human mind. A religious man is one, it is said, who is taken up with objects that no one has ever seen, and which, it is further argued, are unworthy the attention of a rational being. We wish for facts, it is repeated by persons of this way of thinking ; we can have no knowledge beyond the evidence of our senses ; we can believe nothing, except what we have actually seen. The religious man, they contend, is in a great error, because he is not content with that, but wishes to obtain truth from the testimony of his inward nature, as well as from his outward senses.

Now we admit, that remarks like these are correct, so far as they indicate the direction which religion gives to our minds, towards the "things which are unseen and eternal ; " but they are incorrect, as we think, in supposing, that this direction does not lead to as clear and certain truth, as that which is opposed to it. The religious man is, indeed, conversant with invisible objects. His thoughts expatiate in regions, which eye hath not seen, but which God has revealed to him, by his spirit. He reposes as firm faith in those ideas, which are made known to him by his Reason,* as in those facts, which are presented to his notice by the senses. He has no belief that human nature is so shackled and hemmed in, even in its present imperfect state, as to be confined to the objects made known by the eye of sense, which is given us merely for the purposes of our temporal existence, and incapable of ascending to those higher spheres of thought and reality, to which the eternal elements of our being belong.

But, allowing this, it by no means follows, that the religious man is a visionary, in any just sense of that word, because, in the first place, he need not neglect the objects, with which he is at all times surrounded, and which are appropriate to the province of sense, and in the second place, the invisible objects, with which he is conversant, have no less truth and reality, than those which are seen.

The religious man need not see less, in the sphere of the senses, than any other man. There is nothing in his faith in the Invisible, which should blind him to any perceptions, within the sphere of the visible. Indeed, he ought to give his understanding a generous culture, that it may be acute and ready to decide on all objects, that come within its province. One part of his nature is not to be educated at the expense of another. One portion of his existence is not to be sacrificed to the claims of another. The present, with its duties, its enjoyments, and its dangers, is not to be forgotten, amid

---

* The word Reason is used here and throughout these Discourses, not as the power of reasoning, of evolving derivative truth from admitted premises; but in its highest philosophical sense, as the faculty of perceiving primitive, spiritual truth. I am justified in this use of the term by the authority of some of the older English writers, and by a similar use of the corresponding term in the philosophical literature of Europe.

the hopes and prospects of the future. It is a most
pernicious mistake, which leads men to suppose, that
they must give up the interests of this world in order to
prepare for another, instead of making their preparation
for another, to consist in a faithful discharge of all the
claims and trusts of this. The visible is of great importance to every man on earth. Our Maker has made
us conscious of life, in the most intimate connexion with
it. He has surrounded us with objects, addressed to
the senses, on a proper use of which, the religious improvement of life essentially depends. It is our duty,
as immortal beings, not to neglect the present. It is
our duty to provide for its wants. It is our duty to
obtain a wise acquaintance with its necessities. The
truly religious man feels this as much as another. The
enlightened Christian, who understands the spirit of his
Master, and who is resolved to cultivate it, should not be
confounded with the dreaming visionary, who in the
fancied care for his soul, cares for nothing else ; who is
so absorbed in the contemplation of the Invisible as to
lose sight of the important realities before his eyes ;
whose mystic speculations on heaven spoil him for the
duties of earth, like the ancient philosopher, who, in
gazing at the stars, fell into a pit. This is not the
course pursued by the truly-instructed Christian. He
knows that every thing has its place and its importance,
that all duties and all thoughts should preserve a just
proportion among themselves, and if he sees those things
which are invisible, he should give none the less heed
to those which are visible.

But, again, the invisible objects, with which the religious man is conversant, possess as much reality, as
those within the sphere of the outward senses. Do not
call him a visionary, until you have proved that he is

dealing with visions. What if the objects of his attention should be found to have a more substantial existence than any thing which we now see? Do not deem
him a man of a fantastic mind, until you have proved
that he is following phantoms. What if the things that
are not seen, should turn out to be enduring realities,
while the things that appear, are only transitory appear-
ances? It may be that this is the case. We have great
reason to hold that it is probable. Nay, we have the
words of inspiration, declaring that it is a fact. "For
the things which are seen are temporal, but those
which are unseen are eternal." What then are the
unseen realities, to which the Christian gives his faith,
and on which he acts, with as much confidence and
hope, as if they had passed within the boundaries of his
earthly vision?

I. The Christian is conversant, I answer, with an
invisible God. The Mighty Being, upon whom he depends and whom he worships, is infinite, and of course,
incomprehensible. He, who sees all things, is himself
unseen. His existence is of a spiritual nature, and of
course, not perceptible to the eye of sense. The very
idea of God, as that of the Primeval Spirit,—from
whom all things proceed and by whom they are sustained, who is present in every part of his creation, to
receive the homage of the intellect and the heart,—
precludes the supposition, that he can be seen by the
outward eye. That is formed for a different purpose,
organized with different powers, and called to a different service. It is designed to place us in connexion
with the various forms of matter, to reveal to our souls
the beauty of the external universe, and to make us
acquainted with the properties and laws of created
Nature. If it were possible for God to be seen by the

eye, he would be no longer the Being that he is. He would be deprived of the attributes, which make him worthy of our highest adoration and praise. He would no longer be infinite but finite, for our finite senses comprehend only the latter, and ceasing to be infinite, he would cease to be God. The Creator of the universe, if capable of being seen by the bodily eye, would be reduced to a level with nature, would become a material object, and of course no longer God, since God is a Spirit, and only by the pure in heart can he be spiritually discerned. But I would ask, if the fact, that God is invisible, and from his very nature ever must be so, takes aught from the reality of his presence, or from our convictions of his existence ? Is he any the less near to the heart of the good man, than if he could be apprehended with the eye of sense ? Do we not repose as firm a faith in the Being of God, as we do in the objects of nature, which reveal his wisdom and his love ? It is impossible for the enlightened Reason to avoid this. Though the eye cannot see God, the soul perceives him. It does as great a wrong and injustice to its own nature, when it doubts the inward convictions of a Maker and Governor of the world, as if it were to refuse evidence to the testimony of the senses, with regard to the outward universe. The decisions of Reason, which may be regarded as the very essence of the soul, compel us to admit the existence of God, as the ground of our own existence, of an Infinite Being, as the first cause of finite nature, of an invisible spirit, as the origin and support of the visible universe. Deny this idea, who can—he cannot wholly deny his own Reason,—and though he may endeavor to cast it from him, it will again return, its voice will make itself heard, announcing the presence of the Almighty, and he cannot reject the convictions which it brings. Now, it is with this God, whom the eye cannot see, but whom the Reason cannot call in question, that the Christian is conversant. He feels, that it is his privilege to hold communion with the Maker of the universe. He rejoices in the endowments of his nature, which ally him with God, and enable him, on this lower earth, to worship Him who is eternal and unseen. The thought, that God is at all times near to him, is one, which touches his heart with grateful joy; it enlarges his happiness in the hour of prosperity, and mitigates his suffering in the season of sorrow. At all times, he looks to his Father in Heaven, with the assurance, that no needless pang will be inflicted, and no needed good withheld. With the same confidence, with which he trusts in the permanence of the universe, the stability of nature's laws, he trusts in the wisdom of that God, whose Providence is none the less certain, because its source is unseen. And yet such a man would, by some persons, be deemed a visionary. They who suppose that religion is a dream, because its objects lie beyond the sphere of the senses, would regard the Christian as a dreamer, because he worships a God whom he has not seen. But in so doing, he is in fact paying homage to the highest laws of his own being. He is yielding his deepest reverence where his Reason tells him that it is due ; he is conversant with that great reality, which, though unseen by mortal eye, is the ground and centre of all other reality in the universe.

II. Again, the Christian cherishes communion with an invisible Saviour. Next to the God and Father of our Lord Jesus Christ, it is Jesus himself who is the dearest object of his gratitude, his sympathy, and his love. No subject makes a deeper impression on his heart than the character of his blessed Lord. No remembrance touches more powerfully the springs of his best feelings than the remembrance of the love of Christ, who laid down his life, that we might live. He sees in him the manifestation of the Father's glory, the express image of the Divine Perfections. All that we most love and adore in God,—his holiness, his justice, his benevolence and his truth,—is displayed in the person of his Son, and by the spiritual contemplation of that, we obtain the best idea of the Father himself. But here is nothing presented to the senses. None of us ever saw the Saviour of men. We did not know him after the flesh. No material representation could convey to our souls a just impression of his character. Indeed, we obtain so much clearer a perception of him, by bringing his actions in review before the mental eye, that there can scarcely be a material representation, intended to represent the features of his character, which does not fall far short of the conceptions which we had previously formed. Every thing here is addressed to the soul. It is the inward eye, that beholds the glory of Christ. It is to the principle of faith, that his spiritual presence is revealed,—and who can say that it does not make him conversant with a noble object? Who can deny that the recollection of such a being as our Saviour was, calls forth our highest faculties, and introduces us into a region of thought, in which it well befits a man to expatiate? Is the Christian the sport of a vain and idle fancy, when he communes with an unseen Saviour? Is he giving way to a visionary delusion, when he calls up the remembrance of him who became a man of sorrows, that we might be partakers of joy; who tasted the bitter cup of death, that we might drink the waters of life, and opened to us the gates of Heaven, by his own agony on the cross? Is this communion with an invisible Saviour, the delusion of an enthusiast? All the better feelings of our nature declare that it is not. All the homage that is paid at the tomb of departed worth, all the gratitude that is lavished on the benefactors of our race, all the reverence that is accorded to glorious specimens of moral perfection declare that it is not.

III. Again, the Christian is conversant with the invisible powers of his own nature. He is in a state of constant communion with feelings and faculties, that he has never seen. He takes counsel of Reason. He inquires at the oracles of Conscience. He communes with his own heart. He is conscious that he is the possessor of a living soul—of a soul which is to live for ever. He has no more doubt of the existence of his soul, than he has of the existence of his senses. He believes in his Reason as much, nay more, than he does in his eyes. But it is all invisible. Nobody has ever seen the inward nature of man. The researches of the anatomist stop short of it. It cannot be laid open with the knife. It cannot be exhibited for inspection. It is the object of no one of the senses. It is as invisible as the Creator himself. But does any one doubt, on that account, the reality of his inward nature? Can the Christian be charged with folly or with prejudice, because it is his aim to submit the senses to the soul? Can we call in question the existence of the Reason, of the Conscience, of the feeling of moral obligation, because we have never seen them? If we are not aware of their existence, it is because we have never felt their power; and if we have never felt their power, what does it prove with regard to ourselves? If the Christian is guilty of folly, in paying reverence to unseen powers, give me his folly rather than the wisdom of one, who by his own confession, is

3

a stranger to Reason, to Conscience, to a sense of obligation, to the noblest attributes and faculties of man.

IV. Once more, the Christian is conversant with an invisible world. He believes in the existence of a state of being which he has not seen, with as much confidence as in the reality of the world which he now occupies. He has obtained too deep and correct an insight into his own nature, to admit the idea for a moment, that the "be-all and end-all" of man is with the present state. He is conscious of undeveloped powers, which demand an Eternity for their expansion, and he feels sure that God will grant the opportunity, where he has given the capacity. The future world then rises before him, as his final home. His thoughts often dwell upon it, with the deepest interest. There he hopes for brighter manifestations of God. There he expects more intimate communion with his Saviour. There he trusts to enjoy the acquaintance of kindred minds, who have lived in past ages and distant lands, and who in Heaven have become one through Christ Jesus. There are the prophets of the elder world, through whose noble spirits God spake to his people. There are the venerable sages, whose lips dropped wisdom and whose hearts were devoted to truth. There are the white-robed throng of the apostles, with palms in their hands and crowns of glory on their heads. There are the glorious host of the martyrs, who went up by blood and fire, to their Father's throne. These all have obtained the promises. They have crossed the dark river. They have tasted the bitter waters of death. They are before the throne of God, and the Lamb's name is written on their foreheads. Shall not the Christian think of them? Who would prevent him? Who would tear from him those holy hopes, which are the charm and solace of his present existence? Who

would deny him the privilege of indulging in those an-
ticipations, which are demanded by his feelings and sanc-
tioned by his Reason, because they are not laid open to
the eye of sense? He cannot tell, indeed, by any
cold deductions of the understanding, how the dead are
raised up, or with what body they do come, but he believes that the same God, who raised up Christ, will
also raise him from this mortal life on earth, to a higher
life in Heaven. The nature of that life he cannot fully
describe. Its pursuits, he does not know. Its connexion with space and with time, he does not comprehend.
But he feels his intimate connexion with it. He knows,
that compared with it, this life is but a dream—a vapor.
He is sure, that it cannot be far off. Soon will he enter
upon its amazing scenes. Soon will its mysteries be
disclosed to his waiting faith, and a higher consciousness
of existence commence. He does not see that world,
but he expects to meet there beings like himself. How
many have gone before him! How many will be there
to receive him! Angel voices call him from on high.
Angel-hands are stretched forth for his aid. The dead,
who have gone, are living still. The angel-friends who
have vanished from earth are angel-spirits in the presence of God. They speak to his heart, when it is open
to the voices of Eternity. Their spiritual presence is
revealed, as the shadows of earth disappear and the
glories of Heaven draw nigh. And will you say, that
the Christian should not often commune with invisible
realities like these? Will you tell him that because
the prospects of Eternity are shut out from his sight,
they should also be shut out from his heart? Speak,
thou faithful disciple of Christ! Speak, ye, who look up
for rest in Heaven! Speak, pilgrim of earth, as ye behold in the distance the shining walls of the city of God!

Speak, heart of man, that yearns, with desires that cannot be expressed, for a closer union with the Infinite and
the Eternal! Speak! and ye will say, that there is
no worthy object for the Everlasting Soul, but the things
that are unseen—no source of illimitable joy, but the
Infinite Presence of God!

DISCOURSE II.

---

2 CORINTHIANS IV. 18.

" WE LOOK NOT AT THE THINGS WHICH ARE SEEN, BUT AT THE THINGS WHICH
ARE NOT SEEN."

It is a peculiar trait in the character of the Christian, as we have seen, on a former occasion, that he is conversant with objects which are invisible to the eye of sense. He cultivates the habit of communion with an unseen God, an unseen Saviour, the unseen powers of his own soul, and the unseen future, to which he is destined. In my discourse, this morning, I wish to continue the train of thought, in which we have recently been engaged, and to urge upon your minds the importance of attention to the invisible objects, with which we are connected.

I. In pursuing this subject, I would first remark, that the things which are unseen possess the only independent reality. This assertion, I know, is contrary to our usual modes of conception. The objects of sense make so early and so strong an impression upon our minds, that we soon learn to regard them as more real than any others. Our first connexion is with the material universe. We are awakened, in the first instance, to a consciousness of our own being, through the influence which it exerts upon our frames. We learn to know our-

selves, by having previously learned the changes which
we experience from the agency of outward objects. The
universe, with its varied beauty and splendor, is spread
forth in our presence, it addresses every faculty and ex-
cites every feeling, we behold its vast and complicated
changes with reverence and awe, and it is not surprising
that we should regard it as clothed with original and independent reality.   But, in truth, the things which are
seen were not made of things which do appear.   The
material universe is the expression of an Invisible Wisdom and Power.   It has its origin in the will of the Infinite, who has made it what it is, endowed it with all
its properties, impressed it with all its tendencies, as-
signed it all its law s, and by whose energy it is ever
constantly sustained.   The creation in itself, without
reference to the Almighty Spirit from which it sprung,
is formless and without order—a mass of chaotic objects, of whose uses we are ignorant, and whose destiny
we cannot imagine.   It is only when its visible glory
leads our minds to its unseen Author, and we regard it
as a manifestation of Divine Wisdom, that we can truly
comprehend its character and designs.   To the eye of
sense, what does the external creation present?   Much
less than we are generally apt to suppose.   Consider
every thing which we learn from it, merely through our
bodily organization, you will be surprised to find how
small an amount can be summed up.   Deduct all the
pleasure it gives us, through the medium of our higher
nature, all the associations which it suggests to thought
and feeling, all the indications of a spiritual presence
and glory, which its significant symbols reveal to our
souls, and you will find that what remains, is of far less
interest and importance than you would at first have im-
agined.   The outward creation, indeed, exhibits an

ever-changing variety of forms, of colors, and of motions, which excite the perception of beauty and produce intense delight in the mind of the beholder. But what is it that the external eye perceives, when it contemplates this? Merely the different arrangements of matter, the various degrees and directions in which the light falls on the object admired, and the change of position with regard to space. This is all that is seen. The rest is felt. The forms are addressed to the eye, but the perception of beauty is in the soul. And the highest degree of this is perceived, when the outward creation suggests the wisdom of the Creator. Without that, it is comparatively blank and cold and lifeless. It is his existence which furnishes the ground for the existence of that, and connected with Him, as the Primal Fountain of Being, it derives all the reality which it possesses, from his Sovereign Will. How unwise, then, to confine our attention merely to the outward form, and to forget the inward spirit, which it represents! How unworthy of the character of a man, to be so occupied with the mere outside, the dry husk and shell of matter, as to lose sight of the Infinite and Divine Energy, from which it draws the reality of its being.

The things that are seen, moreover, are dependent, in a great measure, upon our own souls. We have another instance, here, of the relation between the visible and the invisible, and the subjection of the former to the latter. It is often said, I am aware, that the soul is dependent for its character and growth, on the external forms of matter, with which it is connected, and that it is greatly influenced by them is a fact, which no observer of human nature can deny ; but it is no less true, that the outward universe is to a great degree, dependent upon our souls for its character and influence, and that by changes in our inward condition, a corresponding change is produced in the objects with which we are surrounded. It is from the cast and disposition of our souls, that external nature derives its hues and conformation. Place two men of different character, in the same outward scenes, how different is the effect which takes place. To one, perhaps, whose heart is tuned to the praises of his Maker, every thing suggests the presence of Divine Wisdom and Love. The voice of God is heard in the rushings of the wind and the whisperings of the breeze, in the roar of the thunder and the fall of the rain; his hand is visible in the glories of the midnight sky and the splendor of the opening morn, in the fierce majesty and might of winter, and in the greenness and beauty of the returning spring; every object is an image of the goodness of God; every sound, a call for his adoration; every spot a hallowed temple for his praise. But to the heart of the other, no such feelings are suggested. He looks coldly on, amid the fair scene of things, in which he is placed. No emotions of admiration or of gratitude penetrate his soul. No sound comes to him from the depths of nature, answering to an accordant sound within the depths of his own heart. He views all that is before him, with a spirit of calculation or a spirit of indifference. Yet he sees precisely the same objects with his companion. The same outward universe is unfolded to his view. The same material sights meet his eye; the same material sounds touch his ear; the same forms and colors and motions, are addressed to his senses. But is it in fact, the same world that is beheld in the two cases? In one, it is a living image, speaking forth the glory of God; in the other, a mute and dead mass of material forms. Whence is this difference? Whence, but from the souls of the two spectators? It is upon the inward condition that the outward reality depends. The visible universe is to us what our invisible souls choose to make it. Here, then, we have a reason for looking at the things which are unseen—for making them the chief object of our attention. In so doing, we become conversant with the primal source of reality. We ascend to the original fountain of Being, from which the streams that flow forth receive their properties and their direction.

II. Again, I would remark, that the things which are unseen possess the only permanent existence. The stupendous masses of matter upon which we repose our eye, appear, indeed, to be imperishable. The solid mountains are girt with strength which seems to defy the ravages of time. The boundless ocean is spread forth, an emblem of endless duration, as well as of unlimited extent. The shining hosts of Heaven arise in their calm beauty, as if they were everlasting. Yet we know that compared with the Eternity of their Maker, they are but of yesterday, and that they might be tomorrow blotted out of existence, while God would remain the same and of his years there would be no end. We can even see the marks of change and of progress, of alternate renovation and decay, on almost every part of the material universe. The ancient mountains fall and come to nought. The volcanic fires that have raged for many centuries are quenched. The vast plains which were once the bed of mighty waters now afford a home to peaceful flocks. And what assurance have we, that the same Omnipotent Will, which at first called the universe into being, subject to the conditions of time and space, may not at length decree its entire destruction? Who can say that the images of ancient prophecy will not receive a literal fulfilment, when the sun shall be turned into darkness, the

stars fall from their places, the heavens be gathered together as a scroll, and the elements melt with fervent
heat? There is no intrinsic permanence in the outward world to prevent such a catastrophe. It is composed of frail materials. It exists in temporary and
changeable forms. It is held together by the sovereign
will of God. And were this great globe itself, with all
that it inherits, dissolved, the Invisible and Everlasting
Spirit would remain unchanged. God would still exist,
in the mysterious perfections of his nature, from Everlasting and to Everlasting.

The human soul, moreover,—that vital and unseen
Intelligence, which animates our bodies, manifests itself
in our actions, and constitutes our true and proper
self, continues the same, although the outward universe passes away. The power, which could quench
the stars, does not touch the soul of man. Its existence is not dependent on the decaying forms of matter,
but it partakes a higher life from Him, who is the source
and centre of all being and consciousness. The hour of
death does in fact annihilate the material world to the
human soul. It dissolves the connexion by which it is
bound to its objects. It destroys the instruments by
which all communication with it is held. It closes up
the avenues through which every notice of its properties
was conveyed to the mind. It spreads a veil over the
objects of sense, so that it is in fact the same as if they
no longer existed. When the eye is closed in that last
sleep, it is as if the light of the sun were put out. When
the ear is sealed in the silence of death, it is as if all
the music of nature were suddenly hushed. To the external senses the outward world exists no longer. The
visible heavens and earth have passed away. But the
soul survives. Its life is safe in the hand of God. It

does not die with the organs of sense, that were but its
servants. It has only changed its outward manifestation, to become the recipient of a new and nobler life.
It has left these heavens and this earth, which our eyes
behold, to be a denizen of a brighter Heaven, a more
glorious abode.

III. I observe, again, that it is upon unseen things,
that the happiness of man essentially depends. Outward objects can do nothing for our happiness, independent of our inward state. It is the unseen condition of our souls that makes us what we are; and upon
this depends our highest welfare and joy. Let a man
be placed amid the brightest splendors of the material
universe. Let all the glories of Heaven and of earth be
unfolded before his eye. Unless he has an inward
sense of their beauty, they cannot give him any happiness. Unless his soul is purified to enjoy their presence, they are like pictures to the blind and music to
the deaf. Suppose that he is ignorant, uninstructed,
the victim of superstition and slavish terror. Suppose
that he has no just sense of the love of God, and cherishes an abject fear of his wrath. All the majesty of
the outward universe will then be inadequate to impress his mind with calm and peaceful reverence. The
treasures of Nature are not sufficient to impart a confiding trust to his soul. He will hear the wrathful
voice of an incensed Deity in every sound. He will
see his frowning face in every changeful aspect of the
sky. He will quail and pant for dread at every new
phenomenon which he beholds. Can such a man be
happy? It is impossible. Can he be otherwise than
miserable? Never. And whence does his misery
arise? From within, from himself. From a diseased
state of the unseen soul. Make that right, you dry up

the fountain of wretchedness that he bears within him. Inspire his soul with a filial love of God, and you make the world a Paradise at once. Let all outward circumstances remain the same, and correct the things that are unseen, you place his happiness on a secure foundation.

And again, suppose that a man is blessed with a great degree of outward prosperity. His lot is cast in pleasant places, and he has a goodly heritage. He enjoys a situation in life that is adapted to gratify all his tastes and desires. His home is crowned with every thing that heart can wish. The course of events glides smoothly on, and every one who sees him remarks on his good fortune. But is this outward prosperity capable of imparting happiness to his soul ? Can it satisfy the deep wants which his nature feels ? Perhaps if you could lift the veil from his heart, you would find him one of the most miserable of men. If he trusts in the external prosperity which he enjoys, it is certain that you would find him without any firm hold on happiness. One evil passion within his bosom is sufficient to poison all his sources of enjoyment. He must have attained to an inward peace, peace with God, peace with his own conscience, peace with his fellow-men, or he cannot partake of the springs of joy that gush up before his own door.

IV. I would add one more consideration. The things which are unseen are more within our power than those which are seen. Man, with all his boasted improvements, has little control over the external universe. The world around us goes on, independent of our agency, without consulting our will. We cannot increase or diminish, to the amount of a single grain of sand, the quantity of matter of which the earth is composed. We cannot alter the time of the rising or the setting of a single star; the glorious constellations of Heaven roll over our heads, as they are impelled in their majestic silence by an unseen hand; and all that man can do is to gaze in admiration or fall prostrate in reverence and joy. This is not his province. But his kingdom is within. His authority is over the hidden world of his own spirit. There he can exercise a rightful and commanding sway. Lord of himself, of the unseen powers of his own being, he can reign there with a more than kingly sovereignty. He can control his inward passions, assuage the tempest of his feelings, still the storms of wild desire. The everlasting lights of the soul are called forth at his bidding, they are dimmed and sullied by his neglect, and upon his own will it depends whether they shine on in their radiant courses or fade in disastrous eclipse. Here is the consecrated sphere, in which his action may be effectual, which he may fill with brightness and purity and joy, or with darkness, pollution and despair. And is it not a greater privilege to be able to move the soul than it would be to reach the sun? Is it not a more blessed destiny to be endowed with power to clothe our spiritual being with light, than it would be to act upon the pale orbs of the starry sky? Is it not wise in us to give the strength of our souls to those things which are unseen and eternal, that we may thus consecrate those which are seen and temporal?

DISCOURSE III.

THE DIVINE ELEMENTS OF HUMAN NATURE.

2 PETER I. 3, 4.

"ACCORDING AS HIS DIVINE POWER HAS GIVEN UNTO US ALL THINGS THAT
PERTAIN UNTO LIFE AND GODLINESS, THROUGH THE KNOWLEDGE OF HIM
THAT HAS CALLED US UNTO GLORY AND VIRTUE, WHEREBY ARE GIVEN UN-
TO US EXCEEDING GREAT AND PRECIOUS PROMISES, THAT BY THESE YE MIGHT
BE PARTAKERS OF THE DIVINE NATURE, HAVING ESCAPED THE CORRUPTION
THAT IS IN THE WORLD."

In these words we have a brief but comprehensive description of the purpose and the effects of the
Christian religion. The blessings which it imparts are
referred to the power of God, as their original cause,
and its ultimate design is declared to be the progress
of men in glory and virtue, so that they should become partakers even of the Divine Nature. You will
observe, from the declarations made by the Apostle,
the profound views which he cherished of the character and objects of the Christian faith. You will perceive how clearly and firmly he regarded it as the
great means, in the divine appointment, of renovat-
ing the nature of man, and preserving him from the corruption to which he was exposed by his condition in the
world. According to his opinion, Christianity was no
superficial system, intended merely to regulate the external conduct, and preserve a decent regard to social

morality among men. It had a far higher aim, a wider purpose. It was designed to take hold of the deepest and strongest principles of human nature, and to bend them all to the practice of goodness and the service of God—to fill the heart with an immortal hope, and to purify it as a holy Temple for the Spirit of God. Neither did the Apostle regard Christianity as a system of abstract speculative doctrines. He had no idea of resorting to it, for an explanation of theological mysteries which the mind of man cannot comprehend, and which exert no influence on the feelings and the life. Peter was no sectarian. He was no framer of systems. He had no love for the discussion of nice and difficult points. It was far from his view to make Christianity a battle-field, or the cross of Christ a standard of contention. He regarded it almost entirely in its profound practical bearings, as a system adapted to produce the most magnificent changes in the heart of man and the fortunes of the world. He saw in it a light, which, once admitted into the human soul, would purify it from darkness and sin, make it conscious of its immortal destiny, and call forth its divine nature into constant and active exercise. How freely does he allude to the capabilities of man, and the power of Christianity to give them their utmost development and energy—how joyfully does he speak of the state of purity and communion with God, into which the promises of the Gospel bring the believer in Christianity—of the progress which he is to make in glory and virtue, even to a resemblance of the Divine Perfection, an approach to the nature of the Infinite Mind. This moral and spiritual state is what Peter speaks of as a plain matter of fact. He holds it up with the strength and simplicity of deep conviction, as the object to which the Christian should aspire

and which the power of his religion will enable him to
attain. Without the slightest approach to enthusiasm
or extravagance in his language, he speaks with great
clearness of the destiny of Christians to become partakers of the Divine Nature.

But, when we first give our attention to declarations of this kind, we are apt to imagine that they
set forth something beyond the reach of human ability.
We look on men as they exist around us, and it is
difficult to form just and high conceptions of their
nature and destiny. We hear of the power of religion
to make them partakers of the divine nature ; and we
at once think of the contrast which is presented by
their actual condition. Can it be possible, it is asked,
that men with the infirmities and the passions, the
exposures and the weaknesses, the temptations and the
sins, to which all are liable, can ever attain the standard of Christianity, and become partakers of the divine
nature ? You see one, it is said, doomed to a life of
constant and wearisome labor. Every hour his hands
must be employed in procuring his daily bread. The
fatigues of his body impede the free action of his mind,
and worn down by incessant toil, he scarcely thinks of
any thing beyond the narrow sphere of his labors. In
some instances, the constant recurrence of the same
pursuits, the unceasing round of corporeal exertion,
benumbs the faculties, and seems to make the man like
one of the machines or instruments with which he is
employed. You ask, if Christianity can elevate such
a man to the possession of the divine nature, with a
tone, which implies that you suppose the thing is
impossible. Again, you see another sunk in the depths
of poverty. He has hardly a shelter for his head, or
rags to protect him from the violence of the storm.

He has become the victim of abject wretchedness, and
degraded in mind and body; the spark of reason and
feeling, which is given to every man at his creation,
appears to be quenched. Can it again be kindled up,
you are disposed to inquire, and the soul which you
have seen cast down, raised to a fellowship with God?
Or again, your attention may be directed to a gross
instance of ignorance and vice. You behold a man,
uninstructed, unenlightened, without feeling, without
principle, dead to the deepest thoughts and best emotions of our nature, and indulging in the worst passions,
without shame and without remorse, and here, too,
you are tempted to ask, Can the divine Image ever be
made visible on such a corrupted object? Can the
God-like ever be impressed, in deep and lasting characters, on a soul so polluted and lost? I am aware
of the difficulty implied in questions like these. I
cannot wonder, that when we compare the promises of
Christianity with the condition of man, our first emotion should be one of incredulity and almost of despair.
That man—man, degraded, wretched and guilty as he
often is—man the subject of such fierce passions and
such fearful sins—should be capable of a participation
in the divine nature, seems to us a boon of such sur-
passing magnitude as to exceed the power of our
comprehension. But the objections that arise at first
sight are the result of a superficial observation. We
must enlarge the sphere of our vision. We must look
below the surface. We must consider man as he is,
in his strength as well as his weakness, in his capacities as well as his infirmities, in his destiny as well as
his condition, in that part of his nature which is of
Heaven, heavenly, as well as that which is of the Earth,
earthy. This broad and comprehensive view of man

will reveal to us a higher order of powers, which elevate
him above what is exclusive and peculiar to him as
man, and connect him with God.   It will show us the
truth and importance of the Apostle's declaration—that
we may become partakers of the divine nature, and
lead us to aspire after that state as the great object of
our existence.

When it is said, that man may become a partaker
of the divine nature, let us be careful to understand
what is meant by the assertion.   We shall otherwise
fall into the region of extravagance and mysticism.   To
be a partaker of the divine nature, is to possess, in
some degree, the qualities which we attribute to the
Supreme Divinity.   Now it is plain that man possesses
many qualities of an opposite character.   With regard
to this fact, there can be no doubt, and there is no
controversy.   These qualities force themselves upon
the attention of every one.   They are exhibited in
the daily experience of life, and we cannot escape
noticing them.   But we must not look merely at one
side of man's nature.   We must not direct our attention so fixedly to certain qualities which it displays,
as to lose sight of others, which are less prominent,
of a contrary character.   If man can become a partaker of the divine nature, there must be a basis for
such participation in his own nature.   If he can acquire
any of the qualities which we attribute to the Supreme
Divinity, there must be an original capacity for their
cultivation.   There must be a foundation to work upon,
or the building cannot be erected.   Let us inquire
further then, into this subject.   Let us see if there is
any thing in the nature of man, which may enable
him to become a partaker of the divine nature—any
capacities, which may be the germ of qualities in his

character, similar to those which we reverence in the character of God.

I. When we examine the nature which we possess, we perceive at once, that it has a power of a remarkable character, which seems to bear some resemblance to one of the divine attributes—the power of perceiving truth. Man has a faculty, which enables him not merely to count, to weigh, and to measure, to estimate probabilities and to draw inferences from visible facts, but to ascertain and determine certain principles of original truth. He sees not merely that one thing is, and another thing is not, that one object of sense is present and another is absent, but that one proposition, relating to abstract and invisible subjects of thought, is true, and another is false. An assertion may be made, concerning an object which he has never seen and never can see,—which cannot be submitted to the cognizance of the senses, and yet he has the power, which enables him to say, with absolute certainty, whether it is true or false. It is this power, by which all science is created. It was the possession of this power in a remarkable degree, which enabled the solitary thinkers, in the retirement of their closets, whose labors have shed the greatest light on science, to make those discoveries, by which the arts of life have been promoted, and aid given in the pursuit of the great interests of society. This power is Reason. It gives us the immediate perception of Truth. It is the ultimate standard, in judging on all subjects of human inquiry. Whatever appears to be true to our Reason, we believe to be true ; whatever appears false to that, we believe to be false. Existing in different degrees, in different men, it is found in some degree in all. There are certain points on which the judgment of all men is alike—certain propositions, which every one would pronounce true, certain others which all would declare false. We are compelled to this by the nature of our Reason. It is not subject to the control of our will. We cannot say, that we choose to have two and two appear equal to five, and therefore they are so in the sight of Reason ; but this faculty exercises its own judgment, announces its own decisions, enforces its own authority, from which there is no appeal. Does not this show, that Reason though within us is not created by us ; though belonging to human nature, originates in a higher nature ; though shining in the mind of man, is an emanation from the mind of God ? Is not the faculty of reason, similar to the wisdom of God ? As he has the power of perceiving the pure and absolute truth on all subjects, has he not endowed man with the similar power of perceiving truth, on a limited number of subjects ? In this respect, then, I believe that the nature of man has powers by which he may become a partaker of the divine nature—may exhibit qualities of a similar character to those which we reverence in God.

II. Again, man has the faculty of recognising moral distinctions. Of two courses of conduct that are presented to his choice, he is able to say that one is Right and that the other is Wrong. He perceives not merely what would be for his advantage, his interest, what will gratify his passions, or promote the happiness of society, but he sees that certain actions, though they might gratify his selfish inclinations, are forbidden by the law of Duty, and he feels an inward obligation to obey that law. Man does not obtain this knowledge through the medium of any of his senses. It is not the result of that part of his nature which calculates and compares. It is not subject to his own will. A man may be tempted to do a wrong action, and may yield to the temptation;—he may turn away his mind from the contemplation of its character, and thus be blind to its real nature;—but, as long as he gives his attention to an action, not blinded by passion, nor warped by prejudice, but in the pure light of conscience, he cannot make the unjust appear to be just, the wrong appear to be right. A voice within speaks, which he cannot but hear, and tells him the character of the action which he is about to perform. It is common to call this voice within us, this conscience which speaks out its clear behests, whether we will hear or whether we will forbear, the voice of God—and is there not a truth of deep significance in the expression? Is not conscience in the human soul, a quality similar to that attribute of God, which makes him the righteous judge of all the earth? Is not conscience, the voice of God, the word of Him who is of purer eyes than to behold iniquity, and who separates between the evil and the good? As God discerns with his all-seeing eye, the real character of every action, so has he imparted to the human soul, a portion of his spirit, which gives it a similar power, and arms the decisions of conscience with a divine authority. Here then, is an element, by the cultivation of which man may become a partaker of the divine nature. Let him reverence his conscience, and it will acquire a power similar to that justice, which we adore in God. Let him listen to the faintest whispers of that voice, which speaks in his moral nature, and he will preserve, in its original brightness, the image of his Maker, which has been impressed upon his soul.

III. Again, man has the power of disinterested Love.
I do not say, how frequently it is exercised. That is not
requisite for the argument I have in view. It is of no
consequence, how many instances to the contrary may
be adduced from the experience of life, to show that its
actual existence is rare. They only prove that the original element, upon which it is founded, has failed of its
proper culture ; not, that it is wanting in human nature.
It is enough to know that the ground of disinterested,
self-sacrificing love is placed within the heart of man,
and we have at once an element, by which he may be
made a partaker of the divine nature. And that this
germ does exist in the human soul, who can deny.?
Has it not been displayed in examples of benevolence,
which had no selfish object in view, but which went
steadily forward to the accomplishment of their purpose,
in the midst of peril and sacrifice ? It was displayed in
the example of Jesus Christ, who so loved the world,—
who was so interested in the spiritual welfare of man-
kind,—so intent on promoting the highest happiness of
the human race, that he forgot himself, forsook every
earthly interest, suffered every outward deprivation,
and at last sacrificed his life, in the cause which was
dearer to him than any personal advantage which
could be desired. It was displayed in the example of
his apostles, whose hearts burned within them for the
promotion of truth, and who laid down every earthly
blessing at the foot of the cross. It is felt by the philan-
thropist, who is ready, at the expense of his tears and
his blood, to alleviate the miseries of the human race.
It is felt by the friend, who would willingly renounce his
own life in behalf of his friend. It is felt by the parent,
who knows that the happiness of his children are dearer
to him than his own, and who would give up every thing

himself to confer it upon them. It is felt by every good
man, who has so devoted himself to a righteous cause,
that he regards his own interests as but chaff and dust,
compared with the promotion of the cause which he
has at heart. And this love is the very essence of the
Divine character. God is Love, and whoso dwelleth in
Love, dwelleth in God and God in him. It is not of
Earth, but of Heaven. It is the great attribute which
binds the Almighty to the heart of Man. The more we
possess of this quality, the more we resemble God. The
germ of it, which exists in our hearts, is the foundation
for our growing likeness to the Creator, and when it is
fully developed within us, we have become partakers of
the Divine Nature.

IV. Once more, man has the power of conceiving of a
perfection higher than he has ever reached. Not only
so. He can make this perfection a distinct object of
pursuit. He has faculties which the present can never
satisfy. After he has done his best, he feels how much
better it might have been done. He can always form
a conception of a higher model, than any which he can
actually realize. And his nature impels him to follow
this ideal standard—not to rest content in imperfection
—to forget the things that are behind—and to press
forward to higher attainments, to diviner excellence.
The artist sees this vision of perfection in his mind, and
attempts to embody it in the materials that are subject
to his skill ; but the result is never equal to his conception, he still imagines more glorious forms of beauty,
than any which he has produced, his soul communes
with an ideal perfectness, that no human hand can ever
call into being. The good man sees this vision of perfection, when he compares himself with what he ought to
be, with the unspotted virtue, which he can conceive, but

which was never realized, except in him, " who possessed the Spirit of the Father without measure." And this power, belonging to the human soul, is another element, by which man may become partaker of the divine nature. It is the germ of resemblance to God. It is intended to lead us on from strength to strength, from glory to glory, in an ever-growing likeness to the Infinite Source of Beauty, and Goodness and Love.

Consider then, my friends, these four principles of human nature, the power of perceiving Truth—of recognising moral distinctions—of exercising disinterested love —and of aspiring after illimitable perfection, and tell me, if we were not made to become partakers of the Divine Nature ? Does not the soul of Man bear the impress of God ? Are we not created to exhibit the Image of our Maker in its divine purity and splendor ? And if such be our destiny, how solemn is our responsibility !—

DISCOURSE IV.

2 PETER I. 3, 4.

" ACCORDING AS HIS DIVINE POWER HAS GIVEN UNTO US ALL THINGS THAT
PERTAIN UNTO LIFE AND GODLINESS, THROUGH THE KNOWLEDGE OF HIM
THAT HAS CALLED US UNTO GLORY AND VIRTUE, WHEREBY ARE GIVEN UN-
TO US EXCEEDING GREAT AND PRECIOUS PROMISES, THAT BY THESE YE MIGHT
BE PARTAKERS OF THE DIVINE NATURE, HAVING ESCAPED THE CORRUPTION
THAT IS IN THE WORLD."

In a former Discourse from these words, I spoke of
the elementary principles in man, by the cultivation of
which he may become a partaker of the Divine Nature ;
namely, the faculty of perceiving truth, of recognising
moral distinctions, of exercising disinterested love, and
of aspiring after boundless perfection. These elements
in the human constitution, you will observe, are merely
the germs, which, under the influence of a higher culture, produce their natural fruit in the character and life.
Because man is gifted, at his creation, with these divine
endowments, it does not follow that they can be developed without appropriate cultivation, or that they will
be actually displayed in the case of every individual.
They need care, exercise, education, or they will remain
unfruitful capacities. Because man has qualities, which
enable him to become a partaker of the divine nature,
it by no means follows, that he is really in possession of
that nature ; but in order to this, he must enjoy influ-

6

ences that are adapted to bring his own nature to the highest degree of perfection of which it is capable. Now the Apostle, in our text, declares that Christianity presents such influences. He regards it as the means appointed, in the Providence of God, for the perfection of the higher nature of man. The purpose of Christianity, in his view, is to elevate the human soul to a resemblance to God, to make it a partaker of the divine nature. But this is accomplished, as we have seen, by calling forth the native powers of the soul itself, not by forcing upon it any constraint or violence from without. The growth of the soul may be compared to the growth of a plant. In both cases, no new properties are imparted, by the operation of external causes, but only the inward tendencies are called into action and clothed with strength. The fragrance of the plant is elicited by the effect of the air, it opens its colors to the descending light, and assumes a form of beauty and grace, according to the secret law of its organization, under the influence of surrounding circumstances. In like manner, the original properties of the soul are revealed, under the influence of external causes, and in the light and strength of the Divine Spirit, which streams forth from the Primal Fountain, on all created things, its divine elements are quickened into life and activity, and it becomes a partaker of the divine nature. Now this influence which the soul needs, to give it a divine life and strength, is imparted in a peculiar manner in the Gospel of Christ. Let it be brought under the power of Christianity, all that it has of the Divine, the Godlike, will be called forth ; its original capacity for religion will become religion in reality, and it will exhibit a true resemblance to God.

I would then invite your attention in the further prosecution of this subject, to some illustrations of the Power of Christianity, in developing the Divine Elements of human nature. In what manner does the Gospel of Christ address the soul of man, so as to give life and strength to those faculties by which he is capable of bearing a resemblance to God ?

I. I answer, in the first place, by the intimate connexion which it establishes between God and the human soul. The sincere and consistent believer in Christ is brought at once to a deep consciousness of the presence of God. He feels, in a manner which no words can express, that he lives and moves and has his being, in the Father of the universe. The more he becomes acquainted with the spirit of the Gospel, the more he sympathizes with the character of Christ, the more he understands the purport of his teachings; the stronger and clearer is his sense of the near and intimate presence of God. No one ever felt this like Jesus Christ. His mind was so filled and penetrated with the consciousness of God within his soul, that he was said to dwell even in the bosom of God. His whole nature was so truly in harmony with the divine purposes, so completely in accordance with the divine will, that he could say what no one else could say, without presumption, "that he and his Father were One." But in proportion as we ourselves become one with Christ, according to the promise which he gave to his disciples, we shall feel in a similar manner, the nearness of God's presence to our souls, and cherish a constant communion with his Spirit. We shall feel our dependence on God. Every thing which we possess will be regarded as his gift. The powers of our physical and our spiritual nature, the laws by which they are regulated, the manner in which they operate, the effects which they

produce, the gifts of the external world, the blessings
and bounties of the social state, the beauty and magni-
ficence of the vast universe, will be to us so many expressive emblems of the presence of God, the visible
Shekinah, through which he manifests his Will, the mystic book, on whose pages we read, in characters of living
light, the inscriptions of Infinite Power and Wisdom and
Love. We shall feel our responsibility to God, in proportion as we yield our souls to the influence of Christianity. Like our Saviour, we shall always endeavor to
do those things which are pleasing in the sight of God.
The desire of his favor will be so strong, as often to
absorb all other motives, and always to control and
regulate them.

The Gospel, moreover, gives us the brightest manifestation of God in the person of his Son. In him we
behold the full splendor of the Father's glory,—the
express Image of his Perfections. The Infinite Majesty of God is softened and brought down to the perception of man, as it is exhibited in Him who possessed our nature and who knew our infirmities. We
commune with God in Christ, in a more intimate relation than when contemplating the works of creation
or the events of Providence. Our hearts are more
deeply touched, a warmer sympathy is excited, and we
feel a more assured faith, that God who so loved the
world, as to give his Son to die for it, will withhold no
needful blessing from those who trust in Him. As we
are thus brought into the presence of God, by the
power of the Gospel, an influence is sent to our souls,
which allies us more closely with Him. All that is
Divine in our nature is quickened by our communion
with the Supreme Divinity. Our holier faculties derive
new life, and we begin to feel that we are, indeed, the

offspring of God, and destined to share more and more in the perfections of his own nature.

II. Again, Christianity acts upon the divine elements in human nature, by the supremacy which it accords to the power of Conscience. It recognises the fact, that we possess a light within us, the quenching of which leaves us in a darkness more deplorable than if the bodily eye were destroyed. This light our Saviour always endeavored to kindle into a brighter flame, to place it, in its divine majesty, within the soul, and to make it the Searcher and the Guide of human conduct. The tendency of all his instructions is to elevate the power of conscience over the earthly passions and impulses of man, to bring every feeling and affection into subjection to its dictates, and thus to invest it with a sovereign authority over our whole souls. The heart of the consistent Christian always yields obedience to the voice of conscience. He follows this, rather than the suggestions of inclination, or the promptings of passion. The natural feelings of man are not, indeed, suppressed within him, he is alive to all the impressions and emotions which belong to our nature, under the circumstances in which it is placed, but all are subject to the control of that voice, which commands with the authority of God. In this way he acquires an increasing conformity to the divine will. He loses, more and more, his affinity with objects that are merely of an earthly character, and obtains a resemblance to the God whom he adores. His nature as a man is refined, its base admixtures are purified, the spirit of God bears rule within him, and he becomes a partaker of the divine nature.

III. Once more, Christianity quickens the divine elements in human nature, by the activity which it gives to the power of Love. It reveals to the heart of man the love of God, and thus inspires it with a kindred sentiment. The Creator of the Universe is set forth in the Gospel as a Being of Infinite Power, united with boundless Love. Nothing is better adapted to fill our own hearts with disinterested love, than the thought, that it is exercised towards us by the Author of our Existence, and the Disposer of our Destiny. The Christian feels that God is Love. He remembers the unnumbered and unmerited blessings he has received from his bounty. His heart is touched with a deep sense of the goodness of God, and expands in emotions of love towards his fellow-men. In the person of his Saviour, he beholds a signal and affecting example of the love of God, and his own love is enkindled by the contemplation. At the same time, the Christian regards his fellow-men in a light adapted to call forth his love. They are children of the same Infinite Father with himself. However degraded their condition, they are of one celestial origin. They are all formed in the Image of the Infinite and the Eternal. They are all in possession of those immortal natures, which emanated from the Original Fountain of Life, and which are as undying as their primal Source. With these views of God, and Christ, and of his fellow-men, which the Christian obtains from his religion, the fountains of love within his heart are unsealed. The power of selfishness is subdued. The principle of sacrifice is quickened. He learns to live for others and is anxious to bestow happiness rather than to receive it. He tastes the blessedness of generous affections, he lives in the exercise of love to man and love to God, and is thus made a partaker of the divine nature.

IV. There is another point which I would notice, in

which Christianity acts upon the better nature of man, and that is the lofty Ideal of Perfection which it presents. We have seen that one of the elements of our nature, which fits us for religion, is the power of conceiving a degree of excellence, which we have not reached. The Gospel of Christ addresses itself to this power, and presents before it a standard, to which it must aspire, and beyond which it cannot pass. It commands us to be perfect, even as our Father who is in Heaven is perfect, and to imitate Christ, who was the brightest type of the divine excellence, that ever appeared on earth. In this way it calls forth the principle in human nature which aspires after perfection, to its most active exercise, and we are thus made to attain a nearer resemblance to God.

From the views which have now been presented, we may learn, my brethren, the real nature and distinct purpose of Christianity. It has been sometimes said, I trust without much consideration, that Christianity is of no utility to man, and that we might as well be without it as with it. But the answer to this objection is contained in the views that have been already stated. Christianity is designed to cherish and call forth the divine elements in human nature, and thus to elevate it to a true fellowship with God. It is the instrument in the gradual education of the human race, for its highest advancement in all that is pure and noble, just, righteous and godlike. All the advances that man has made, have been the effect either of Christianity, or of a spirit similar to that which it contains, and the more extensively its influence is diffused, the more completely does he attain that participation of the divine nature, to which he is destined.

We perceive, moreover, from this subject, the true manner in which the evidences of Christianity are to be understood. It is the correspondence between the divine spirit of Christianity, and the divine spirit in man, that gives it the power of commanding a just and rational belief. If we are insensible to the divine spirit of Christianity—if its real character, as breathing the same spirit which we love and adore in God, has not been revealed to our minds, we can have no clear and distinct perception of its truth. On the other hand, if the divine spirit in our own hearts has been quenched—if the elements in our nature, which ally us to God, have never been called into life and action, we can have no hearty faith in Christianity. As face answereth to face in a mirror, so the Divine in the Gospel answers to the Divine in the heart of man. Let Christianity be clearly understood—let the heart of man be pure and alive—and they rush forward to meet each other,—each as bearing the Image of God, and emanating from his Holy Spirit.

Finally, I remark, that the best understanding as well as the clearest evidence of Christianity is to be found in our own experience. We think much of the evidence of sight—and justly, but the evidence of consciousness is more. We think we fully understand a subject which we have examined with our eyes, but there are some subjects which we understand the best, from feeling them with our hearts. So with Christianity. If it has quickened all the purest and most generous sentiments of our nature—if it has called forth all those qualities in our hearts, which bear the greatest resemblance to the divine character—if it has raised us to communion with the Infinite Spirit of the Universe, and made us partakers of his nature, we need not that any one should instruct us with regard to its claims, for we know and feel, and have the testimony in our own hearts, that it is indeed the wisdom of God, and the power of God unto salvation.

DISCOURSE V.

JOHN XVI. 30.

" BY THIS WE BELIEVE THAT THOU CAMEST FORTH FROM GOD."

IN Dr. Paley's celebrated statement of the argument
for the existence of God, he adopts a mode of reasoning
which may be applied with equal clearness and force,
to the evidences of Christianity. Suppose, says he, that
in crossing a heath, I pitched my foot against a stone,
and were asked how it came there, I might answer,
without exposing myself to the charge of absurdity, that
it had been lying there for ever ; but if, on the other
hand, I had found a watch, and the same question were
asked, I should be obliged to answer that it was the
work of an intelligent and skilful artificer. The argument, you perceive, rests upon the fact, that corresponding products are to be referred to similar causes. The
stone alluded to by Dr. Paley, possessed none of the
properties, to which we are accustomed in works of
art. There was no curious organization, no complicated machinery, no adaptation of means to ends, no fin-
ished and delicate workmanship, and hence there was
no reason for ascribing its production to the skill of an
artisan. It bore no resemblance to the products of his
ingenuity. It possessed nothing in common with them,

which would authorize the supposition that it was the work of the same hand. The watch, on the contrary, exhibited all the qualities which we are used to observing in the products of intelligence and skill. It was clearly made for some purpose, it bore the marks of evident design, and all its curious arrangements plainly fitted it for the production of the intended effect. It accordingly resembled, in its essential properties, those works which are admitted to be the fruits of ingenuity and art, and it would therefore be a fair procedure to refer the watch itself to a similar cause. No one, who has ever read Dr. Paley, can have failed to be struck with the simplicity and force of this argument, in its application to the great topics of Natural Theology, but I wish, at this time, to direct your attention particularly to the principle, which is at the bottom of it. The principle is, that when we admit a given product to be the work of a certain author, a second product similar to the first must be admitted to be the work of the same author. In the schools of art, for instance, the productions of Michael Angelo are acknowledged to possess a distinctive character, which it would be difficult for a connoisseur to mistake. Now if a painting were to be discovered, among the remains of the old masters, bearing all the characteristics of his style, with such power and originality as to preclude the idea of a modern imitation, it would be an irresistible conclusion to infer that he was the author. It would be impossible to suppose, that two different works, which bore the same impress of peculiar and inimitable genius, could have proceeded from dissimilar sources.

Now I propose to apply this principle to the evidences of Christianity. If we can compare Christianity with some other product, which is admitted to be from God,

and find that it possesses the same characteristics, we
shall have a strong proof, that Christianity itself is also
from God.   The principal difficulty in such a discussion
is, to discover the term of comparison and to point out its
coincidence with Christianity.   If we had the work of an
artist—to revert to my former illustration—it were easy
to take that as the standard of comparison, which should
be applied to other works under examination.   But
what, it may be asked, what work do we possess, admitted to be from God, which is of such a nature that
it can be used as a standard in judging of Christianity?
Where shall we find the term of comparison, by proving
Christianity equal to which, we shall prove Christianity
to be from God?   I answer, it is to be found in the
higher nature of man.   If we can lay our finger upon
any thing, in this broad universe, and say that it is from
God, it is his spirit within the human soul—the fruits
of which are those elements in our constitution, by
which, according to the Apostle's expression, man may
become a partaker of the Divine Nature.   If there is
any created thing, which displays the seal of Divinity,
and bears the impress upon its face that it comes from
God, it is the higher nature of man—the faculties of
Reason and Conscience,—the power of conceiving and
aspiring after Divine Perfection.   This truth has been
recognised among all nations, and in every age.   The
universal testimony of human nature has borne witness
that there is a spirit in man, and that the inspiration of
the Almighty hath given him understanding.   It is expressed in different languages that the voice of conscience is the voice of God, and that all truth, clearly
perceived by the reason of man, is from the Supreme
and Eternal Source of truth.   We are authorized, then,
in assuming, that the higher nature of man is from God,

in the sense not merely that it is created by him, for in that sense the brute and the vegetable, the unfeeling marble and the lifeless clod are from him ; but that it possesses in some degree the qualities which we attribute to God, just as the stream partakes of the qualities of the fountain from which it flows.

If then the dictates of Christianity and the dictates of our higher nature are identical, admitting that our higher nature is from God, we have a powerful argument that Christianity is from God also. This argument I shall endeavor to set forth and sustain in the present Discourse.

My proposition is, that Christianity coincides in its dictates with the higher nature of man.

My first point will be to show what I understand by Christianity, and then, to illustrate its coincidence with our higher nature.

I. When it is said that Christianity coincides with the higher nature of man, it is of the utmost importance to the success of the argument that we obtain a correct and clear idea of what Christianity really is. This is by no means so easy as many suppose. Among the prevailing errors of the community, which together with much truth, we have inherited from former ages, few are more deeply rooted than those which concern the nature and character of Christianity. Were it always viewed in its true light, as it existed in the mind of its Author, and was exhibited in his teachings and his life, I do not say that it would never have an enemy, but I am certain, that to every man whose soul retained the image of God, it would appear as his brightest and most glorious manifestation on earth. Christianity has been grievously misrepresented and misunderstood. The light shineth in darkness, and the darkness comprehendeth it not.

1. By Christianity is not to be understood, the whole of the contents of the Bible. This is a very common idea, but it is very incorrect. When Christianity is spoken of, the attention is often directed to the entire mass of matter contained in the Bible, as if it were identical with Christianity itself. The effect of this is great confusion and embarrassment of thought. For want of a proper discrimination on this point, the whole subject becomes complicated, and often eludes every attempt to present it in a clear and intelligible light.

We speak, for instance, of the reasonableness of Christianity. But the mind of the hearer, instead of turning to the pure doctrine of Christ, is often directed to some fact or narrative in the history of the Old Testament which appears to him unreasonable, and because we are speaking of one thing, and he is thinking of another, the force of the argument is lost, and no conviction is produced.

We speak of the beautiful and heavenly character of Christianity. But instead of the attention being led to the system of religion and morality which our Saviour taught, some transaction belonging to the childhood of civilization, but recorded in the Bible, is suggested to the mind, and secretly presented in opposition to the argument.

We speak of the divine origin of Christianity. But the want of discrimination, to which I allude, leads men to exhibit passages of Scripture, which had reference to the early fortunes of the Jewish people, and only a remote connexion with Christianity, and ask, if we can suppose that such passages, or such scenes as they describe, are to be attributed to a divine origin?

The error, in every case of this kind, arises from the primary mistake of confounding Christianity with the whole of the contents of the Bible. The truth on this subject is, that the Bible contains a complete record of Christianity, but it also contains much additional matter. It is not entirely taken up with Christianity, nor with religion. It presents a history of the inspired men, to whom early revelations of God were made, but it is not, itself, the revelation, nor the immediate result of that revelation. It contains sufficient to satisfy us, that God has made a revelation of his will to his children—that holy men of old spake as they were moved by the Holy Ghost ;—and in many instances, it records the words which were thus spoken, but at the same time, it is not filled with them, but gives an account of many subjects of a different character. The Bible is not one book, but a collection of books, composed in various languages, at different times, by numerous authors, and hence there is no book in the world, the contents of which present a greater diversity of matter. It contains the primal traditions of the human race which were embodied by the great Lawgiver of the Jews, in the language of poetry and song, and transmitted to the most distant generations of the chosen people ; the history of a nation, whose character was peculiar and whose fortunes were wonderful, from whom succeeding ages have inherited some of their most valuable treasures of civilization, learning and religion ; the remains of philosophy and literature, to which the first efforts of the human mind gave birth, and which have served as the foundation of a future and better progress ;—all these are contained in the Bible—all these are important, interesting, and of great price, but they are not Christianity, and they should no more be confounded with it, than the light, golden clouds which precede the rising of the sun, with the sun itself.

2. By Christianity, I observe, again, we are not to understand all the reasonings and illustrations which the sacred writers employ with regard to it. These are, indeed, intimately connected with Christianity, but they are not to be mistaken for the spirit and essence of Christianity itself. In reading the Scriptures, we should always distinguish between the great truths which the writers intend to convey, and the peculiar forms under which those truths are expressed. In judging of Christianity, we should separate between the essential principles, which its original teachers set forth as the substance of the gospel, and the collateral ideas and allusions by which these principles are enforced. The sacred writers, for the most part, received the message which they delivered from Christ himself. They heard the doctrines of truth and righteousness from his lips, and their minds were inspired with the spirit of God to understand them. The truth which they received in this manner was from heaven. But it was deposited in earthen vessels. It was committed to the keeping of men, who though illumined with a ray of light from above, yet saw through a glass darkly, who knew but in part and who prophesied in part. This truth was expressed in human language, for the plain reason that it was addressed to human minds. It was illustrated by comparisons taken from objects which were then familiar, by allusions to opinions which were then prevalent, and by adaptations to habits of thought which formed a part of the national character of those to whom it was addressed. The logic, by which the arguments in its favor were carried on, bore the impress of those times. All that was external, the whole costume in which the divine truth was arrayed, partook of the peculiarities of the individuals to whom it was committed; but the

truth itself—the pure spirit of Christianity was essentially separate and distinct. When we speak of Christianity, then, let us be understood as speaking, not of all the reasonings and illustrations of the sacred writers in regard to it, but of the real doctrine of our Saviour himself.

3. Neither, in the third place, are we to understand by Christianity, the theological systems contained in the creeds and confessions of faith, which have been adopted in most of the great churches of Christendom. These for the most part have been the result of dim conceptions of Christianity, and of imperfect views of truth in general. They have been produced not by an enlightened study of the Scriptures, in order to ascertain their exact meaning, but by the desire to bring the testimony of Scripture into accordance with some favorite system of speculation. Men wished to philosophize on the simple truths of Christianity, to explain what Christ left unexplained, to clothe the expressions of feeling and sentiment with the precision of logical ideas, to give to the language of emotion and poetry, the rigid forms of a scientific system, and in this manner, the confessions of faith have been framed, which with the intention of placing Christianity in a clearer light, have drawn around it a veil of darkness, that conceals its divine beauty from its friends, and makes it an object of bitter hostility to its foes. But think not, my brethren, that such documents are a correct expression of the divine spirit of our religion. Do not look into the copies of those worn and tattered parchments, for a living record of our faith. Go not to those symbols, whose words were imprinted on your memory, before your minds could comprehend their meaning, for your ideas of Christianity; they do no

8

justice to the heavenly truth proclaimed by Jesus
Christ ; they set up a cold monumental image in place
of the breathing spirit of our Saviour, so that when you
look to them for bread, they give you only a stone.

4. None of the points, to which I have now alluded, is to be mistaken for Christianity. They must
be separated from our conceptions of Christianity, if
we would obtain a correct idea of its nature and character. We must exercise our minds to make a just
discrimination between what is essential and what is
adventitious, what is the spirit and what is the letter,
what belongs to Christianity itself, and what is only
casually connected with it. We are to understand by
Christianity, the doctrine which our Saviour taught.
In him, it pleased the Father, that all fulness should
dwell ; in his person, the fulness of the divine character ; in his instructions, the fulness of divine truth.
Whatever he taught in his precepts or in his life, in his
briefest hints, or his copious expositions, we regard as
the essence of Christianity. The views of religion,
which he cherished himself, are the views of religion
which every Christian should cherish ; the spirit which
he breathed, should be breathed by his followers ; the
faith which he taught himself, and about which there is
no difficulty, should be the faith for which we contend
as the substance of revelation, " the glorious Gospel of
the Blessed God."

It may be asked, how are we to ascertain the real
doctrine of Christ, when such diversities of opinion prevail with regard to it ? I answer, by adopting those
principles, which have received the general assent of
believers in Christ. With regard to the essential points
of Christianity, there has in fact been no dispute. Men
have contended about words and expressions, but there

has been a general agreement with respect to the fundamental principles of Christianity. What our Saviour intended to be essential he made plain. He stated it so simply as to leave no room for dispute. Upon other points, which he left untouched, men have divided and engaged in controversy. Now if we pass by all these, and go to the instructions of our Lord himself, we shall find a great mass of truth, which all Christians agree in receiving, and it is this truth which corresponds to the higher nature of man, and forms the essence of Christianity. Ask any man who ever read the Gospels, what was the purport of our Saviour's teachings, and he will say, the spiritual worship of God, the cultivation of purity of heart, the exercise of universal love, and the hope of immortal life. The truths, contained in these principles, make out the substance of the Gospel, and it is for their divine origin that we contend, when we contend for the divine origin of Christianity.

Once more, do you ask how are we to ascertain the real doctrine of Christ ? I answer, by the rational interpretation of the language of the sacred writers. Most of the differences of opinion which prevail, have arisen from an incorrect view of the meaning and application of the words of Scripture. Illustrations of a principle have been taken for statements of facts, the traditional opinions of the writers for the teaching of revelation, and the glowing figures of poetry for the accurate expositions of science. Hence men have lost sight of the true doctrine of our Lord. Hence many theories of merely human speculation have been mistaken for the inspired revelations of Christianity. The only way in which we can avoid these difficulties, is to explain the language of the Bible on the same principles of good sense which we apply to the explanation of any other composition. We shall then go from the letter to the spirit. We shall comprehend the mind of Christ Jesus, and find that we arrive at the same conclusions which have already been mentioned—conclusions in which all Christians agree, about which there can be no dispute.

II. In the further prosecution of my argument, I am to show, that Christianity, as thus understood, coincides with the higher nature of man, which is admitted to be from God, and that, consequently, Christianity itself is also from God.

1. My first remark is, that Christianity corresponds to the higher nature of man in its revelations of God. Suppose that the religion of Jesus presented views of the Divine Being, which are repugnant to the. clearest ideas of justice and humanity, it would be impossible to receive them as coming from God. They would contradict the testimony of his Spirit within our nature. They would bear no resemblance to the divine qualities which connect man with God, and we should be compelled to reject them, as at war with his attributes. But this is not the case with regard to Christianity. Its revelations of God coincide with the dictates of the higher nature of man. The voice of Jesus, which speaks to us of our Father in heaven, is identical in its utterance with the voice of a cultivated reason and conscience.

Christianity teaches, in the clearest manner, the existence of an Infinite and Spiritual Being, who. is the Fountain of all life, the Author of all blessings, and the Disposer of all events. But this truth is asserted with equal clearness by man's higher nature. Wherever the noblest powers of man have been signally manifested, the purest homage has been paid to the great fact of a Supreme, Spiritual Existence. The brightest lights that have ever appeared in the world, have bowed with the

lowliest reverence before the Infinite Source of uncreat-
ed light. The loftiest minds have ever been the most
earnest to seek the Original Mind. They have been
conscious of their divine nature. They have felt their
need of divine illumination and aid. They have yearn-
ed for near and intimate communion with the great
Father-Spirit, from whom their own spirit was derived.
The heart and the flesh, the most holy emotions and the
most active powers of man's nature, in every age, have
cried out for the living God ; the human soul, in its
purest flights, has testified that God is our Father, that
from him we came and to him must return.

The higher nature of man has ever acknowledged the
divine power, as the origin of every blessing. Hence
the institution of sacrifices and other external forms of
worship, in every nation. God was felt to be the giver
of all good. The ripened harvest which waved in beauty before the reaper was from the Infinite Spirit. The
clustering tendrils of the vine were nourished by his
power. The delicious fruits of the earth were matured
by the elements which he had made. The graceful an-
imal was created by him. How appropriate, then, to
set apart a portion of that, which was most prized by
man, in honor of the Sovereign Giver. This was the
dictate of the better nature of man, in an early stage of
cultivation, and the same sentiment has been cherished,
under every degree of progress ; the human soul has felt
its connexion with God, and sought to express its emotions by the observance of external rites. The same
spirit, which Christianity breathes, has existed in man ;
the same revelations which that sets forth in a perfect
light, had been presented in partial glimpses ; the same
God, whom our Saviour proclaimed, had been found by
the higher nature of man, so that all which is divine in

his soul responds to that which is divine in Christianity; it acknowledges it to be from a kindred source, and perceives in it the power and spirit of God, on which it depends itself.

And as the revelation of God in the Gospel, is responded to by the divine elements of human nature, so these have not been able to attain any knowledge of their Author, superior to that which Christianity presents. The highest idea of God which it is possible to form, does not surpass that which was announced by Jesus Christ. The mind of man, with its divinest powers, can approach no nearer to the true conception of God, than it is brought by the Prophet of Nazareth. Through him we have the most intimate access to the Father. Whatsoever we ask in his name we shall receive. And if then the testimony of Christianity thus completely coincides with the testimony of our higher nature in relation to God, is it not just to conclude, that they are from the same source—that our Master was inspired with the same wisdom and power from above, which created the human soul?

2. Again, Christianity coincides with the higher nature of man, in ascribing supreme authority to the decisions of conscience. In this respect, they both utter the same language. They agree, in such entire and consenting harmony, that it would be impossible to suppose they had their origin in dissimilar sources. They are so identical in the demands which they make for the supremacy of conscience, that it would be no less unwise to ascribe them to different causes, than to refer the beams of light, which fall upon the earth, to different suns. Our Saviour instructs us to follow the voice of conscience at all hazards—to do what we believe is right, at any sacrifice—to pluck out our eye, or to cut

off our hand, even to part with life itself, rather than
sin against the law of duty, which is written upon our
hearts. He allows no compromise between right and
wrong. He tolerates no degradation of conscience to
the power of impulse and passion. And this is precisely what is commanded by the higher nature of man.
There is a voice within us, which we admit to be from
God, that tells us to scorn the guilt of a wrong action.
We can read the decree written upon our hearts, to do
our duty and trust in God. This decree has been recognised by all noble and generous natures. They have
felt its authority. They have yielded to it their obedience. How many have reverenced so far their higher nature, that they would rather suffer, rather submit
to torture, rather die, than sacrifice a principle or vio-
late a duty! How many have forsaken every worldly
advantage in the cause of truth! How many have gone
forth cheerfully to the dungeon and the rack, the scaf-
fold and the cross, rather than dishonor the voice of
conscience and prove recreant to the law of God within
their souls! In such exhibitions of human nature we
perceive a divine power. We admit that the light
which guides them is light from Heaven. And can we
see the perfect coincidence between the revelations of
the Gospel and the voice of God in human nature, and
not acknowledge them to be of a kindred origin? Did
not the same Being who wrote the law of duty on the
heart of man, inspire his Son, who set it forth with such
clearness and force?

3. Still further, Christianity coincides with the higher nature of man, inasmuch as they both inculcate the
exercise of universal love. Suppose that a religion were
presented to us, which commanded us to hate each other, and on every occasion to pursue our own interests

at the expense of our neighbor's happiness. Suppose
that it permitted us to take every advantage of the
weakness and ignorance of our fellow-men, to defraud
them when we saw fit of their property, to injure them
in their persons, to forsake them in their distress, and to
cherish every evil passion and sentiment towards them,
could any external evidence make you believe that such
a religion was from God? Could you be convinced,
even though one should rise from the dead in its attes-
tation, that it was inspired by his divine spirit? Would
you not rather, on the contrary, reject a religion of such
a character, almost without examining its claims? Would
you not feel yourself justified in saying that it could not
be from God, although the voice of an archangel should
declare that it was? But why would you adopt this
course? Because you could not do otherwise, in accordance with your own nature. It would be doing
violence to the better part of yourself to admit that such
a system could be the revelation of God. And the reason clearly is, that it does not coincide with the divine
elements of the soul, which every man regards as the
standard of truth. Our higher nature tells us, to love
and live in peace with all men. It strengthens the
bands of love, which unite men together, as a company
of brethren. It inculcates the duty of reverence towards
our fellow-beings, as children of God. It tends to break
down the barriers of birth and of fortune, of differences
of opinion and varieties of condition, which divide the
heart of man, and to combine the scattered members of
our race, in the great brotherhood of humanity. This
is a consummation for which the noblest minds have de-
voutly longed in every age. The higher nature of man
has inspired him with the godlike sentiments of charity
and peace, of toleration and universal love. Christian-

ity does but echo back this voice. It declares in responsive tones to the cry of humanity, that we are all brethren upon the earth, and that our highest duty to God is to do good to one another. It sets forth the broadest principles of philanthropy. It inculcates the most liberal spirit of tolerance and kindness. It wars with every narrow prejudice. It plucks up the roots of hostility and ill-will from the heart of man. It breathes the most enlarged and generous sentiments, and would make them universal. In this respect, it corresponds to the most divine elements of human nature. If then, you would reject a religion of an opposite character as unworthy of God, have you not a decisive proof that this religion is from God? You compare it with the bright manifestation of God, which the sentiment of human love affords, and perceiving their identity, is it not the fairest reasoning to conclude that they both have one Father—that they are equally from God?

4. Again, Christianity coincides with our better nature, in its commands to aim at spiritual improvement. The purpose of human life has ever been an object of anxious inquiry with thoughtful men. The result of their meditations has been recorded in their works. The wisdom, which they accumulated from the experience of many years and the exercise of profound reflection, is treasured up in their writings, and has come down, embalmed in its own undying fragrance, to the present time. And what testimony does it give? What is the confession of those noble spirits who have pondered most deeply on the mysteries of life, and attained in their own characters the purity of heart which allied them most nearly with God? Consult the pages of wisdom which have been transmitted to us, from the prophets of Judea and the sages of Greece, you will find

9

they all agree in the declaration that virtue is the highest good of man,—that resemblance to God is the noblest aim of life. They counted it a base thing to be
under the dominion of the meaner passions. They
scorned the slavery of the senses, and fought for the freedom of the soul. They regarded no evil so great as
sin. They dreaded no bondage so much as the bondage of the evil appetites. They wished to elevate
their nature above the level of the brute, and cultivate
its godlike capacities. Improvement in all that is generous and noble-minded, all that is just, pure and hon-
orable, all that is benevolent toward man and devout
toward God, was considered by them the only aim,
worthy the highest efforts of a man. This is the testimony of the master-spirits of all ages, whose thoughts
have outlived the ravages of time. The poet has given
utterance to these truths in the sweet voice of song, the
philosopher has clothed them in the venerable forms of
reason, the moralist has lent to them the winning graces
of persuasion, and the orator has enforced them with all
the majesty of eloquence. It was here that the heart
of man spoke out. Here his better nature has testified
to itself and to all others, that it was not made for the
degradation of vice, the foul dominion of base passions.
Here has been uttered forth in strains that ring loud
and clear upon the soul of ages, that there is a divinity in man, which must seek its kindred source. And
how powerfully does Christianity respond to this voice
of our higher nature ! It tells us, what we had been
told before, but never with so much force, to scorn the
empire of our baser appetites and place our affections on
lofty things. It reveals to us the Infinite Source of
Perfection, manifested in the person of our Lord, as
the object, to which our souls should aspire, which

we should ever try to imitate. The highest elevation
of our spiritual nature, the victory over ourselves and
over the world, a moral union with God, is the great
purpose which it presents to our endeavors. How complete the coincidence with the divine elements in human nature! Is not the proof direct, that they both
have one Father? Can I believe that God is the Creator of my soul, the inspiring breath of my reason and
my conscience, and not believe, at the same time, that
the mind of Jesus drew inspiration from his spirit?

5. I have time to mention but one other coincidence
between Christianity and our higher nature. I refer to
its indications of a future life. Whenever the higher
powers of human nature have been quickened by culture,
man has felt that this world was not his final home.
The secret instincts of his heart have told him that he
possessed something which death could not destroy.
The hope of Immortality may not indeed have been
fully developed, a cloud has rested upon the prospects
of the future, and no messenger has appeared to an-
nounce glad tidings of the spirit-land ; but yet in the
noblest natures, with whose thoughts we are permitted to
commune, at this distance of time, an instinctive yearn-
ing has revealed to them the sublime hope of humanity,
and led them to cling to the faith that they should not
die entirely, as the dearest heritage of man. In such
minds the voice of God in the endowments of our nature spoke though in whispers, and taught the same great
truth, which our Saviour placed in the brightest light.
This voice was heard in the soul of the Grecian martyr,
who amid the gathering darkness of his narrow cell
calmly discoursed on that land of light, which he hoped
to enter after death ; it spoke comfort to those generous
spirits, who in times of public woe held it sweet and

noble to die for their country ; and it now addresses
the pure in heart, who are not blessed with the Christian faith, assuring them that this is but the infancy of
a life which is to be matured in other scenes. We
here find the testimony of our higher nature. And to
that testimony the Gospel of Christ responds. It tells
us clearly what man had hoped and wished before. The
divine message of the Gospel corresponds to the divine
instincts of the soul. It explains and strengthens them.
It confirms this vast hope which the human understanding would never have conceived, but which the Divine
Spirit in the Reason of man has anticipated, that we shall
live for ever ; that death is but one event in the mysterious cycle of our conscious existence, a link in the great
chain of circumstances which connect us with the universe and with God. On this point, the most interesting which frail man can contemplate, the Divine in our
nature and the Divine in the gospel completely harmo-
nize. The seal which God has impressed upon the
human soul, agrees with that which is borne on the face
of Christianity. Were they not both enstamped there
by the same hand ?

It is thus, my hearers, as the image of God is displayed in the divine elements of our nature—that a
similar image is presented in the revelations of the
Gospel. Shall we not recognise the likeness ? Are
not the spirit which breathes in the human soul and the
spirit which breathes in the religion of Christ, brother-
spirits, that have come down from their native heaven
to conduct the creatures of earth to their home with
God ? Yes, they are of a kindred origin, they know
and love each other, and as soon as the spirit of man
becomes conscious of its affinity with God, and beholds
the same image in Jesus Christ, it utters what it cannot

but feel,—By this we know that thou camest forth from God. We are thus made free from the heavy burden of doubt, and enabled to embrace a faith, that will satisfy the soul—a faith, that is not merely a form of lifeless words, but the strong conviction of our hearts—a faith, that is so incorporated with the deepest elements of our nature, that no earthly power can destroy it—a faith, that will sustain us in the temptations of life, and reveal to us an unchanging home in the hour of death.

DISCOURSE VI.

MATTHEW V. 8.

"BLESSED ARE THE PURE IN HEART, FOR THEY SHALL SEE GOD."

An interesting truth is expressed in this declaration of our Saviour, entirely in accordance with the train of thought which I have recently attempted to set forth, and which may form an appropriate close to the discussion in which we have been engaged. I have endeavored to show, that there are elements in the constitution of man, by which he may become a partaker of the Divine Nature, that the design of Christianity is to call forth and quicken these elements in the human soul, and that the correspondence of Christianity with all that is divine in our nature, proves it to be of a kindred origin—proves it to be from God. I wish this morning to shew that the presence of God is perceived by these divine elements of human nature, and with the discussion of this subject, I shall terminate the series of connected discourses to which I have invited your attention.

"Blessed are the Pure in Heart," said our Saviour, "for they shall see God." It is evident from this expression that it is to the heart, or inward nature of man, in a state of purity or freedom from subjection to the lower passions, that the presence of God is manifested.

When it is promised that we shall see God, we cannot suppose that the contemplation of the person or the form of the Infinite and Invisible is intended, in the same way in which the objects of sense are brought before the human eye, for we know that God is a Spirit, and that by a spiritual perception only can he be discerned. But as we have a more distinct impression of objects, which we see, it is natural to represent a clear perception of the presence of God, by an image taken from the faculty of sight. The meaning of our Saviour then is, that the presence of God is revealed most fully to the Pure in Heart. And this fact is in perfect harmony with a great law of our constitution, which presents one of the most interesting aspects of human nature. The law to which I allude is, that every perception of external objects takes place, according to a corresponding arrangement in our inward constitution. Thus the light falls upon the eye, and received by a most delicate and curious organization, conveys the perception of color to our minds. The sun might exist as the fountain of light, as it now does, and pour forth its streams over the earth, but, were there no corresponding provision in the inward nature of man for the perception of the outward objects, the beauties of nature would be a lifeless blank, the variety of colors, of forms, of motions, in the universe, would be without significance, and the lavish bounty of Providence apparently bestowed in vain. The perception of light depends upon the purity of our vision. The beautiful objects which it creates are revealed to a corresponding power within. Let that power be weakened, darkened, or destroyed, the enjoyment of light is taken away— and when that power is annihilated, it is the same as if the sun were blotted out of existence. You may apply this process of reasoning to all the faculties of man and

the objects with which they are conversant. The laws
of sound are in accordance with the construction of the
human ear. The most thrilling music is without effect,
when the inward faculty to which it is addressed is de-
ficient. Let the ear of man be sealed, the melody of
nature would in fact be silenced. These considerations
apply directly to the subject of our present discussion.
As the light of the sun is revealed only to purity of vision, so is the presence of God to purity of heart. As
we are provided with a mental organization to perceive
the harmony of sounds and the beauty of colors, we are
also provided with faculties to perceive the presence of
God, the operations of his Divinity. As light and sound
are addressed to portions of our nature, expressly
adapted to their recognition, so the Divine Presence in
the Universe, is addressed to the divine elements in our
nature. If they are preserved in purity, God is recognised by the Soul. If they are weakened by passion,
darkened by sin, or sunk into degradation amid the temptations of life, the light of God's face is hidden, his Presence is apparently withdrawn, he goeth before us but
we see him not, he is on our right hand but we do not
perceive him. It is to the Divine in human nature,
that the presence of God is revealed, and of course, if
that is quenched, we have no powers by which to ascend to our Maker. We may possess other faculties
in great perfection—our understanding may be clear, our
discernment acute, our faculty of calculation almost in-
fallible ; but if the divine elements in our nature—if
Reason and Conscience, the sentiment of Love and the
thirst after Perfection, are debased, we have no more
power of perceiving God than the blind man has of perceiving the colors of the most brilliant painting. He
may hear it described if he has good ears, and thus form

some imagination with regard to it, but he does not see it, has no perception of its qualities, no admiration of its beauty. If, then, we would perceive the presence of God, so that he may be as distinct a reality to our souls, as if he were an object of sense, we must cherish those elements of our nature which ally us directly with him. We must preserve, in their original purity and power, all those qualities which resemble the attributes which we adore in God, and which present the intrinsic characteristics of Divinity. These alone can exercise the consciousness of their celestial origin. They are streams which partake of the properties of the fountain that they flow from, with the power of tracing themselves back to their primal source. The Pure in Heart are those in whom these pure elements are alive. They have not yielded to the base dominion of worldly passion. They have not quenched the divine spark within their souls by indulgence in sin. They live in the habitual exercise of Love, of Reverence for the behests of Conscience, of obedience to the law of Duty, of aspirations after boundless Perfection and a near communion with the Divine Mind. They cultivate and give strength to all those qualities, which bear the stamp of coming from God, and the claim of sovereign authority. Perfect, indeed, they are not, they feel that they have not yet attained, they are conscious of great deficiency, for the light of Heaven is ever attended with the shadows of earth, but yet their affections are placed on divine things ; they live in constant communion with the Invisible, they have not effaced the Image of God from their inward nature, and possessing this Purity of Heart, they behold the Father, they see God.

I. The Pure in Heart see God within their own souls. I mean by this, that the consciousness of their own nature reveals to them the presence of the Eternal. The human soul is the great argument for the Being and perfections of God, and if we are insensible to this, we can have a living faith in no other. The qualities, of which we may become conscious in our own nature, lead us directly and irresistibly to the idea of a God, from whom they proceed. As soon as we become acquainted with our own souls, we perceive that they are dependent, limited, finite, but at the same time endowed with powers, that command with absolute authority, with capacities for boundless improvement, and aspirations after an approach towards Infinite Perfection. Whence has the soul these faculties ? Who stamped upon it these ideas, or made it susceptible of receiving them ? Surely not itself. Its endowments are not the result of its own will. They were not acquired in consequence of any exertion of its own. It found itself in possession of them, when it first awoke to a full consciousness of its own nature, and felt itself impelled by a resistless force, to manifest and exercise them. They can be traced to no other source than to the Eternal Fountain of Truth and Good. But these endowments of our nature cannot be perceived, when they are sullied and debased by the indulgence of earthly passions and the foul corruption of selfishness and sin. They exist, but the signs of their existence are buried up, they present no manifestations which the consciousness can appreciate, and as God is not seen in them, he is not seen with a clear eye and a strong faith in any region of the Universe. This is the cause of our defective trust in God and our mournful insensibility to his presence. We look for the indications of his Being, at too great a distance from ourselves, instead of finding within our own hearts, such marks of his presence as would make him a felt and living reality. Until we have become alive to the elements of Divinity in human nature, which compel us to perceive the existence of an Infinite and Eternal Divinity, we can have no deep and intimate communion with God, no sense of his presence so distinct and vivid, as to be like seeing him face to face. But this sense is given to us, my hearers, in proportion to our Purity of Heart. Just as far as we preserve the Image of God with which we were created, in its unsullied brightness, we shall be conscious of its possession, and as we behold this Image within our souls, we shall see God, who is its Original. We shall be filled with a deep reverence in contemplating the mysteries of our own nature. The operations of our minds in the pursuit of Truth, the sympathies of our hearts in the exercise of affection, the holy yearnings of our nature at the Idea of the Infinite and the Perfect, the majestic authority of Reason, the solemn voice of conscience, the sublime hopes that thrill through our bosoms when our friends pass away on the bed of death, the visions of Immortality that hover round our spirit when we reflect that unto all men it is appointed once to die,—these, and similar scenes, which are presented on the inward theatre of our consciousness, will all be to us divine revelations of God. We shall see in them the presence of our Father. He will pass before the eye of our thought, and we shall no longer say, shew us the Father and it sufficeth us, since we have known and seen him, within our souls.

II. The Pure in Heart, again, behold God in the various events of life. If they have been led to a living faith in his Being, by a consciousness of his presence within their souls, they will see him in every circumstance of their existence. Their whole experience,

filled with the recollections of his goodness and the
symbols of his wisdom, will reveal to them the Providence of their Father. Life will not appear to them
without purpose and without profit ; but they will
regard it as a portion of their being, which the love of
God has appointed, and for which they are responsible.
They accept it with all its conditions, and endeavor to
spend it as under the eye of Him from whom it
was received and to whom it must be resigned. All
its changes, they feel, are the result of causes which he
holds in operation ; all its blessings, the fruits of that
exhaustless goodness which he always exercises ; all
its trials, the appointment of his wisdom which sees
every thing, which is never darkened and which never
errs. Are they permitted the enjoyment of prosperity ?
They feel that it is from God. The smiles of his love
are seen around their prospects, giving a new and
brighter joy to their blessings. Are they surrounded
with friends, whose intercourse delights their hearts,
and in whose sympathy they find the highest solace
and support,—they remember that it is God, who has
given them their intellect and their affections ; and in
these endowments of their nature made the richest
provision for their happiness. The ties which bind man
to his brother-man ; the necessities of life which unite
heart with heart and soul with soul ; the social rela-
tions, with the deep and still fountains of joy, which
they open to the pilgrims of earth and all the blessings
which flow from seeing in the face of a man the heart
of a brother, are referred to God as their primal cause,
while they brightly reveal his presence and his love.
Has adversity, on the other hand, marred the happiness
that had been vouchsafed,—have the lent gifts of Divine
Providence been recalled,—here, too, the Pure in Heart

behold the hand of their Father, and bow before the
Sovereign Will which controls the universe. Blessed
are the Pure in Heart—blessed indeed—for in the
darkest events of life, they see the light of heaven,—in
the most painful allotments which they suffer, the Infinite Wisdom of God,—in the heaviest shocks of affliction,
the arm of a Parent outstretched to bear them to his presence on high. Blessed are the Pure in Heart, for they
shall see God. Blessed indeed is that pure-hearted
Christian, whose fellowship is with the Father of the
universe, for in the most fearful trial that disappoints his
hopes, he sees the benign appointment of God, and re-
ceives it as his most holy will. Blessed is that pure-
hearted parent, who has put his trust in Him who is the
God of all the families of the earth; for when the lovely
objects of hope and promise that gladden his happy fire-
side, are smitten by the cold hand of disease, and he
watches over the breathing life of his earthly idol as it
grows fainter and fainter, until the last pang has been
borne and the last sigh been heaved, he then feels that
God has not left him alone, he sees even in the dark
messenger of the grave, the spirit-hand that bare an
immortal to the skies—he hears with the last low moans
of pain and death, the spirit-voice from eternity, saying,
earth to earth and dust to dust ; but, thou undying child
of God, thou image of the Eternal ! come thou hither, to
Heaven, which is thy native place—to God, who is
thy home !

III. The Pure in Heart, once more, see God in the
works of creation. To their eye, the vast universe is filled
with symbols and proofs of the divine presence. They
walk thoughtfully through the mysterious paths of creation ; every step they take furnishes him with new
objects of reverence and love, every discovery of

science reveals to them new evidences of the wisdom and
power of God. A religious physician once told me,
that he could never look upon the lifeless remains of a
fellow-being, inured as he had been to the spectacle,
without the feeling of deep and solemn awe. The
earthly tenement of the immortal spirit, so fearful and
marvellous in its construction, bore the marks of a divine hand, and brought him into the immediate presence
of God. This was the natural result of such a manifestation of heavenly wisdom on a pure heart. The
same effect is produced by all the works of God on
those who have preserved the Divine Image within their
soul. Nature to them is no longer silent but vocal
with the praises of her Maker. Her solemn hymn, ascending from every spot on this broad earth and re-
sponding to the melody of the skies, is heard by them
as they commune with their own hearts and are at
peace. They see the glory of God inscribed on the
face of every created thing. The ancient mountains,—
those old fastnesses of strength,—become to them the
Horebs and Sinais which God has girt with power and
from which he speaks to his people. All the trees of
the wood are like the cedars of Lebanon which reared
their lofty branches in honor of God. The humblest
flower that spreads its modest colors to the sun is like
the Rose of Sharon which reminded the pious Hebrew
of the goodness of his Maker. To them the whole
earth is filled with the glory of God and his praise is
re-echoed from the sounding sea. The freshness of
morning and the stillness of night, the piercing blasts
of winter and the fervid sun of summer, the genial
promise of the spring and the glorious fulfilment of the
autumn, the most distant star that shines and the frail-
est insect that lives,—all are revelations of that Spirit-

ual Presence which surrounds the world, both when we sleep and when we wake ; they are the inspired Prophets of God's will, the holy oracles of his wisdom, the speaking interpreters of his goodness and power. While these revelations pass unheeded before the heart that is lost to itself and wedded to sin, they are received by the Pure in Heart as angels from the Divine Presence, they acknowledge them as the expressive symbols of his love, for they see God in all and all in God.

IV. Finally, I would remark, that the Pure in Heart behold the presence of God in the revelations of the Gospel. They see the glory of the Father in the Person of his Son. There are some minds, who think it unwise to direct the attention to the manifestations of God in Nature, lest it should weaken our interest in his manifestation in Christianity. But it appears to me, that the more clearly we see God as he is revealed in our own souls and in external Nature, the more clearly shall we see him in Christianity. I cannot conceive of any opposition between the God of the Universe and the God and Father of our Lord Jesus Christ. Nature and Truth are from the same Being, the God of Nature and the God of Truth are one. And the same Purity of Heart which perceives God in the world within and the world without, will perceive him also in the Gospel of his Son. For it finds there the same Truth which it had recognised before,—nay, the full-orbed Sun of Truth, of which it had caught before only faint and feeble glimpses. Christianity corresponds to all that is divine in our own nature and in the external Universe, and if our eyes have been unsealed to behold the glory of God in the one, we cannot be blind to his presence in the other. The man of a pure heart and clear insight will see that the Gospel of Christ contains the same elements of Divinity, which he worships under every form in which it is manifested, he will see that in its whole spirit and essence, it is holy, heavenly, Godlike ; and with a faith, as firm as that which he reposes in his own being, he will believe in Jesus Christ, for he sees the presence of God in the revelation of his Son.

My hearers, I have imperfectly set forth the truths, to which I have asked your attention, but let me entreat you to make them the subjects of your own deep and thoughtful reflection. One hour devoted to meditation on the sublime and mysterious significance of these simple words " Our Father in Heaven," may give you more light, than many hours applied to the instructions of the pulpit. Would you know God, first know yourselves. Keep your souls pure as the temples of divine love. Cultivate the spirit of constant prayer. Walk humbly with God in every duty and in every trial. Let your affections be placed on things above. Exercise the spirit of Heaven while you are still strangers and pilgrims on earth. Acquire a true Purity of Heart and you shall see God.

THE END.

DISCOURSES

ON THE

PHILOSOPHY OF RELIGION.

ADDRESSED

TO DOUBTERS WHO WISH TO BELIEVE.

BY GEORGE RIPLEY.

"A true philosophy in the learned class is essential to a true religious feeling in all classes."

COLERIDGE.

Boston:
JAMES MUNROE AND COMPANY.

1836.

WS - #0135 - 100122 - C0 - 229/152/5 - PB - 9781330213445 - Gloss Lamination